RAINY RAINY SATURDAY

by
**JACK
PRELUTSKY**

pictures by
**MARYLIN
HAFNER**

GREENWILLOW BOOKS, New York

Greenwillow
Read-alone

Library of Congress Cataloging in Publication Data
Prelutsky, Jack.   Rainy rainy Saturday.   (A Greenwillow read-alone book)
Summary: Fourteen humorous poems about the pleasures and pains
of a rainy Saturday.   1. Children's poetry, American.
[1. Rain and rainfall–Poetry. 2. Humorous poetry.
3. American poetry]   I. Hafner, Marylin.   II. Title.
PS3566.R36R3   811'.5'4   79-22217
ISBN 0-688-80252-4   ISBN 0-688-84252-6 lib. bdg.

For my parents
J. P.

For L. S. L.—not just
a fair-weather friend
M. H.

CONTENTS

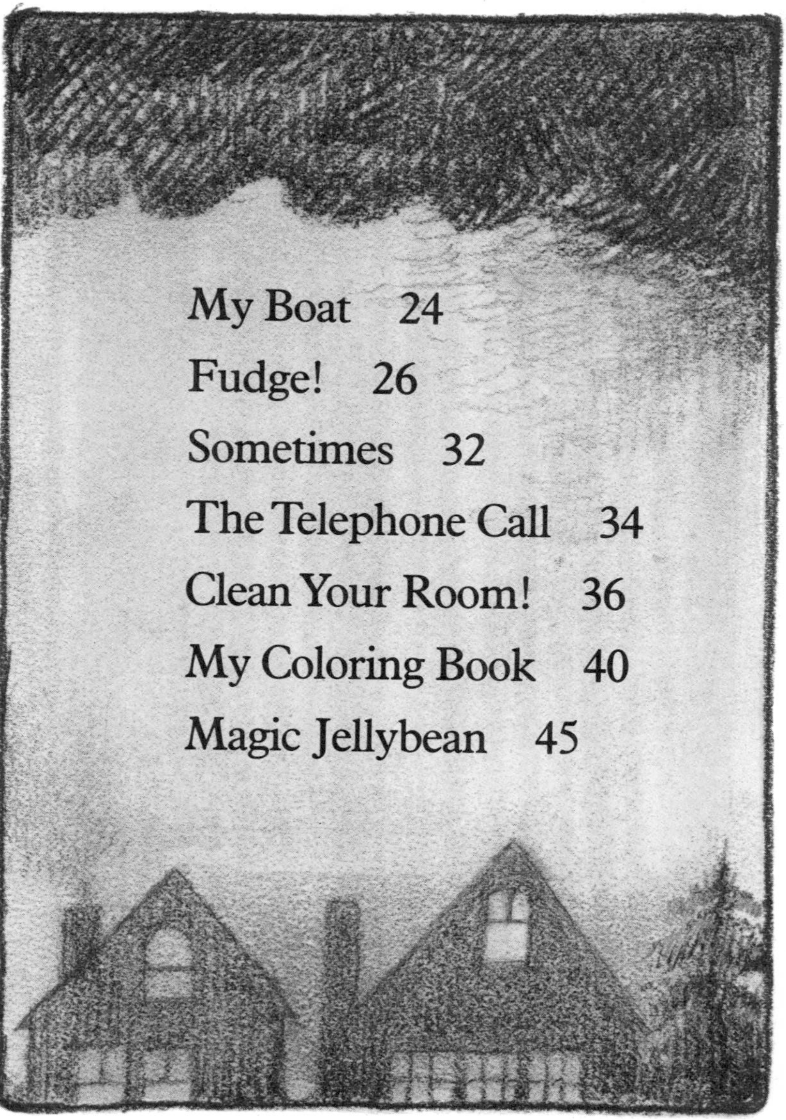

RAINY RAINY SATURDAY

It's Saturday
and what a pain,
no school today
but lots of rain,

and Mother tells me
when it pours,
"The weather's bad
so stay indoors."

I'd rather go
out in the yard,
but no! it's raining
much too hard,

so I will stay
inside and play
this rainy
rainy Saturday.

SOMERSAULTS

It's fun turning somersaults
and bouncing on the bed,
I walk on my hands
and I stand on my head.

I swing like a monkey
and I tumble and I shake,
I stretch and I bend,
but I never never break.

I wiggle like a worm
and I wriggle like an eel,
I hop like a rabbit
and I flop like a seal.

I leap like a frog
and I jump like a flea,
there must be rubber
inside of me.

WHISTLING

Oh, I can laugh and I can sing
and I can scream and shout,
but when I try to whistle,
the whistle won't come out.

I shape my lips the proper way,
I make them small and round,
but when I blow, just air comes out,
there is no whistling sound.

But I'll keep trying very hard
to whistle loud and clear,
and someday soon I'll whistle tunes
for everyone to hear.

MY CREATURE

I made a creature
out of clay,
just what it is
is hard to say.
Its neck is thin,
its legs are fat,
it's like a bear
and like a bat.

It's like a snake
and like a snail,
it has a little
curly tail,

13

a shaggy mane,
a droopy beard,
its ears are long,
its smile is weird.

It has four horns,
one beady eye,
two floppy wings
(though it can't fly),
it only sits
upon my shelf–
just think, I made it
by myself!

15

SPAGHETTI! SPAGHETTI!

Spaghetti! spaghetti!
you're wonderful stuff,
I love you, spaghetti,
I can't get enough.
You're covered with sauce
and you're sprinkled with cheese,
spaghetti! spaghetti!
oh, give me some please.

Spaghetti! spaghetti!
piled high in a mound,
you wiggle, you wriggle,
you squiggle around.
There's slurpy spaghetti
all over my plate,
spaghetti! spaghetti!
I think you are great.

Spaghetti! spaghetti!
I love you a lot,
you're slishy, you're sloshy,
delicious and hot.
I gobble you down
oh, I can't get enough,
spaghetti! spaghetti!
you're wonderful stuff.

20

CHOCOLATE MILK

My chocolate milk tastes better
when I sip it through a straw,
I think it's even wetter
when I sip it through a straw.

With one end in the chocolate milk,
the other at my lips,
I drink up every single drop
with little tickling sips.

TICK TOCK CLOCK

Tick tock,
tick tock,
something's hiding
in the clock,
a thing that makes
a ticking sound
and helps the hands
go round and round,
a thing that can't
be very tall
to fit inside
a place that small.
Tick tock,
tick tock,
something's hiding
in the clock.

23

MY BOAT

I took some wood and wire
and I built a little boat,
then I put it in the bathtub
to see if it would float.

The mast was half a pencil
and it had a paper sail,
and a yellow plastic sailor
stood on watch beside the rail.

It sailed the bathtub ocean
as my fingers stirred the tide,
till I made the waves too heavy
and it crashed into the side.

My little boat tipped over
and with scarcely any sound,
the yellow plastic sailor
tumbled overboard and drowned.

FUDGE!

Oh, it poured and it rained
and it rained and it poured,
I moped round the house
feeling lonely and bored,

till Father came over
and gave me a nudge,
and said with a smile,
"Let's make chocolate fudge."

Then he gave me a bowl
that we filled to the brim,
it was fun making fudge
in the kitchen with him.
I stirred and I stirred,
but I wasn't too neat,
I got fudge on my hands,
I got fudge on my feet,

I got fudge on my shirt,
I got fudge in my hair,
I got fudge on the table
and fudge on the chair,
I got fudge in my nose,
I got fudge in my ears,
I was covered all over
with chocolate smears.

When the cooking was done,
Father wiped off my face,
and he frowned as he said,
"What a mess in this place!"
He was not really mad
and did not hold a grudge,
and we both ate a mountain
of chocolate fudge.

31

SOMETIMES

Sometimes I simply have to cry,
I don't know why,
I don't know why.
There's really nothing very wrong,
I probably should sing a song
or run around and make some noise
or sit and tinker with my toys
or pop a couple of balloons
or play a game or watch cartoons,
but I'm feeling sad,
though I don't know why,
and all I want to do is cry.

THE TELEPHONE CALL

I was mad and I was sad
and I was all upset,

I couldn't go outside to play,
the weather was too wet.
But then my best friend called me up
with lots of things to say,

we made each other giggle,
I felt better right away.

When you can't think of things to do
and the rain won't ever end,
it's nice to have a telephone
to share things with your friend.

CLEAN YOUR ROOM!

"Clean your room!" my mother said.
"Sweep the floor and make your bed,
    pick up all those bits of clay,
    put those books and toys away."

"CLEAN YOUR ROOM!"
   she yelled at me
   when I kept playing quietly,
   but again I disobeyed
   and ignored her, and still played.

"CLEAN YOUR ROOM!"
my mother roared
even louder than before.
She was mad!
She stamped and glared,
I got just a little scared.

"Clean your room!"

she whispered then
softly, softly, and so when
my mother handed me the broom,
I said O.K.-and cleaned my room.

MY COLORING BOOK

When I fill in my coloring book,
how wonderful the pictures look!
I make things how I wish they were,

like leopards white and lavender,
and purple penguins, pea-green goats,
and elephants with orange coats,
yellow calves and rainbow roses,
black giraffes with silver noses,

forests thick with scarlet trees,
swarms of bright blue bumblebees,
zebras striped with gray and pink,
a golden crow, a lilac mink.

I color all the rabbits red
and give a moose a turquoise head,
everything's my special way—
coloring's fun on a rainy day.

MAGIC JELLYBEAN

I was wide awake at bedtime,
not a yawn was in my head,
so I pleaded with my parents
not to make me go to bed.

I grumbled and I whimpered
but I knew I couldn't win,
so I put on my pajamas
and my parents tucked me in.

Now underneath my covers
I'm a deep-sea submarine,
searching in the darkness
for a magic jellybean.

I'll find it and I'll bite it
and I'll wish with all my might
for rainy rainy Saturday
to disappear tonight.

I'll wish for sun tomorrow,
for the clouds to float away,
so that Sunday won't be rainy
like this rainy Saturday.

JACK PRELUTSKY was born and raised in New York City but now lives in Seattle, Washington. His popular books for children include *The Queen of Eene*, *The Snopp on the Sidewalk*, and *Nightmares*–all ALA Notable Books–and *It's Halloween*, a Greenwillow Read-alone Book, illustrated by Marylin Hafner.

MARYLIN HAFNER studied at Pratt Institute and the School of Visual Arts in New York City. She has illustrated several Greenwillow Read-alone Books, including *Mind Your Manners* by Peggy Parish, *Camp KeeWee's Secret Weapon* and *Jenny and the Tennis Nut*, both by Janet Schulman, and *Mrs. Gaddy and the Ghost* by Wilson Gage. Ms. Hafner lives in Cambridge, Massachusetts.